Table of Contents

Chapter 1: Virgo Personality Profile

Ruling Planet: Mercury

Symbol: the virgin

Element: earth

Quality: mutable

Traits: active, adaptable, analytical, anxious, capable, cautious, clean, clever, conscientious, critical, detail-oriented, diplomatic, emotionally reserved, frugal, fussy, hardworking, health-conscious, helpful, humble, intellectual, introverted, logical, modest, patient, perfectionistic, practical, reliable, skeptical, talented

Active

Typical Virgos are very active (it is rare to find a lazy Virgo). Chronically restless and driven to do productive, useful things, Virgos find activity far more relaxing than sitting around, so they are less likely than those of other signs to suffer from health problems caused by a sedentary lifestyle.

Virgos spend nearly every waking moment working, doing volunteer work, making or fixing things, cleaning, taking care of others, or exercising, and when they do allow themselves any leisure time, they typically seek out books, television shows, movies, or podcasts they can learn from or they do arts, crafts, or building projects, depending on personal interests.

Virgos feel lazy if they are not doing something worthwhile at all times even though they tend to achieve far more than most people over the course of any given day. They take a negative view of people who sit around doing nothing and tend to be more compatible with active, energetic types.

Enforced inactivity is very stressful for Virgos, so they have trouble resting when sick. When they are ill or injured, Virgos often force themselves out to work or to do household tasks and exercise rather than taking to their beds and resting.

When socializing, Virgos prefer to engage in active pursuits such as hiking or walking with friends, doing crafts together, playing sports or games, working on a project, or anything else that involves doing or creating something.

Adaptable

Although Virgos like to have things in their homes a certain way, they are adaptable in other areas of life. Naturally pragmatic, they usually move on quickly after a tragedy or the end of a romance. This does not mean they are cold-hearted; Virgos care very deeply about people, but they understand that there is nothing to be gained by wallowing in misery and they are far too pragmatic to engage in prolonged mourning. Life must go on, and Virgos are very good at getting on with things in the wake of tragedy or the midst of hardship.

Virgos are also good at adapting to new environments (or, more accurately, adapting environments to their preferences in such subtle ways that others do not notice the influence Virgos exert over their surroundings and routines). Because they are unsentimental, Virgos are usually willing to move to new places for practical reasons, leaving their hometowns behind.

Virgos are also mentally adaptable. While others may cling to ideas or belief systems even when the evidence stacks up against them, Virgos will abandon an assumption or an ideology when strong contrary evidence is presented. A Virgo would rather be accurate than right, so Virgos tend to be fair-minded when evaluating evidence and willing to concede a point if proven wrong.

Analytical

Virgos have analytical minds, so they are good at figuring things out. Many like word games and crossword puzzles or brain teasers, and some have scientific or mathematical talents.

Critical thinking and problem solving are particular Virgo strengths. Virgos will not take things on blind faith; instead, they apply reason to make their assessments of situations, people, and belief systems, and to find solutions to difficult problems.

Because they are analytically minded, Virgos often do well in school and pursue lifelong learning on their own after graduation. They require plenty of intellectual stimulation, and they will quickly grow bored with those who cannot provide it.

Anxious

Virgos are prone to worrying and obsessing over things, which can lead to anxiety, obsessive-compulsive thoughts and behaviors, chronic anger, or depression. They have trouble quieting their racing minds and letting things go, so they can fall into mental traps in which rumination triggers negative emotional states.

Virgos overthink things. They often mull over unpleasant possibilities or past events for hours on end or second-guess themselves when they were right in the first place. They cause themselves unnecessary stress due to a combination of perfectionism, obsessive thinking, and fear of making bad choices or offending others.

The best treatment for Virgo anxiety is physical activity. Virgos who are very physically active are far less likely to suffer from obsessive-compulsive disorder, generalized anxiety disorder, panic disorder, social phobia, hypochondria, depression, or chronic anger.

Capable

Most Virgos are highly competent. They have good work ethics and do not promise more than they can deliver.

Exacting Virgos learn how to do things properly rather than muddling their way through. They read directions and instructional books or take classes to make sure they do things correctly.

Virgos tend to be very good with the practical aspects of life. They do not typically let things slide (for example, allowing their homes to become disaster areas or failing to pay their bills). Well-organized, responsible, and hardworking, they usually achieve what they set out to do and manage their lives better than most.

Cautious

Virgos are naturally cautious. This often manifests as avoidance of physical risk (Virgos will take calculated risks, but they will not do reckless things on impulse). If

Virgos do choose to do dangerous things (for example, skydiving), they will be very conscientious about checking gear and doing everything else they can to reduce the risk.

Virgos tend to be wary of new people, situations, or activities. They do not like to try new things without doing plenty of research beforehand to assess the risks and benefits. As a result, they are rarely spontaneous and dislike impulsiveness in others

Virgos are also careful with money. Inclined toward financial pragmatism, they are sensible about spending and saving, and they do not like to blow their cash without anything to show for it.

Virgos tend to be cautious in love as well. They do not like to show vulnerability, so they hang back, waiting to be sure that the other person is trustworthy before opening up.

Those who wear their hearts on their sleeves may view Virgos as cold, but Virgos are actually very caring and supportive once they have spent enough time with a person to develop trust. They just prefer not to emotionally invest in people until they are sure they will like them.

Clean

Virgos have a reputation for fastidiousness. It is rare to find a Virgo who is lax about showering or washing clothing. Virgos also tend to keep their homes neat and clean, and some have germ phobias that cause them to shower and wash their hands excessively.

Virgo cleanliness is at least partially attributable to health-consciousness. Virgos have an interest in health and wellness, and they tend to be very careful about issues such as food safety and contamination.

Clever

Virgo is among the cleverest signs of the zodiac. Quick-thinking and eager to learn new things, Virgos are good problem solvers and they can make unusually accurate assessments of situations and people. Because they are unsentimental, their impressions of others tend to be realistic rather than clouded by emotion.

Virgo cleverness can be applied for good or bad purposes. Positive Virgos will use their quick minds to help others, gravitating to professions or volunteer work where they can find new ways to improve the lives of people or animals. However, negative Virgos will use their cleverness to exploit others.

Conscientious

Only Capricorn can match Virgo in conscientiousness. Virgos have a strong sense of duty and a good work ethic. They are reliable, and they value this trait highly in others as well.

Virgos have little tolerance for those who cannot be counted on to do what they promise or show up when and where they say they will. Because they are unwilling to spend time with people who do not meet their standards, they are selective when choosing friends and partners and quick to abandon those who prove untrustworthy or irresponsible.

Hardworking Virgos finish what they start and have no trouble staying motivated. They cannot understand people who abandon projects to wander off in search of something new or take a careless, laid back, or otherwise unprofessional approach to work and hobbies.

Virgo conscientiousness can become so extreme that it tips over into obsessive-compulsive behavior, which can manifest as excessive checking to see if the stove is off, the doors are locked, etc.

Virgos may also have difficulty leaving anything when it is good enough. Instead, they obsessively attempt to perfect every detail even when others would be satisfied with things as they are. A big challenge for Virgos is learning to accept imperfection.

Critical

Virgos are naturally critical, and this trait can have both positive and negative manifestations. On the plus side, Virgos tend to be discerning and hold themselves and their work to high standards. As a result, they produce work of higher-than-average quality and seek to improve themselves throughout their lives. However, their tendency to be critical can have detrimental effects on their relationships and self-esteem.

When the Virgo tendency to be critical is turned outwards, Virgos nitpick, nag, and judge others. They may hold other people to impossibly high standards and drive them crazy with their relentless criticism.

However, Virgos more often turn their critical focus inwards, berating themselves obsessively for slight or imagined failings and becoming anxious or depressed as a result. They may negatively evaluate everything they do, feeling that nothing they produce or achieve will ever be good enough, or obsess over minimal to nonexistent flaws in their character or appearance.

Virgos have trouble being kind to themselves and learning to love themselves as they are. Imagining how they would treat a friend with similar issues can be helpful, as they are usually kinder and less critical with others than they are toward themselves.

Detail-oriented

Virgos have a knack for detail work and sorting and organizing information and objects. They often worry about small details and may excessively structure their lives, plan out their vacations down to the tiniest elements, organize their belongings to an obsessive level, or be chronically dissatisfied with everything they do because they cannot live up to their own impossibly high standards.

Virgo detail orientation can also manifest as a compulsion to collect facts. Virgos enjoy learning and systematizing knowledge, so they often have an interest in trivia. Some become intensely focused on a particular topic while others just love random, interesting facts.

Diplomatic

Virgos are among the most diplomatic signs of the zodiac. They dislike conflict and prefer to talk about things rationally rather than fighting about them.

Virgos tend to keep their opinions to themselves when those opinions are likely to trigger conflict. Their desire for peace and good relations is stronger than their need to be right, and they are too pragmatic to use win-at-all-costs strategies.

Because they are diplomatic, Virgos tend to get along well with others. If they dislike someone, they just avoid that individual or slip quietly out of the relationship rather than confronting the person directly (unless they have no choice). Virgos are far too sensible to pick fights unless other elements in their natal zodiacs incline them to be more reckless and feisty.*

---

* The natal zodiac refers to the positions of the planets in the sky at the time of birth. Important influences in the natal zodiac include the sun sign (the one most people know), the moon sign, and the rising sign (also known as the ascendant). Other elements in the natal zodiac can influence how the sun sign is expressed. For example, a Virgo with Aries or Leo rising will be feistier; more reckless, impulsive, and combative; and less diplomatic than a typical Virgo.

Emotionally Reserved

Virgos are emotionally reserved by nature. They favor logic and rationality over blind faith and intuition, and they dislike emotional drama.

Virgos are quick to escape from relationships and friendships with those who make scenes in public or initiate long, drawn-out, teary discussions about feelings (most Virgos will make an exception for those who are genuinely depressed, anxious, or ill, showing sympathy and patience in these cases, but they are aggravated by people who incorporate emotional drama into their day-to-day lives without good reason).

Virgos are slow to warm up when they first meet people. They are cautious about showing their feelings, taking time to observe and determine whether others are trustworthy before opening up. This can make Virgos appear cold and unfeeling, but the real problem is that they feel far too much when they do let others into their private worlds, so they are not inclined to trust until they are sure of the other person.

Because they do not usually show emotion, Virgos are very cool under pressure (at least overtly), which makes them great to have around in a crisis. They are willing and able to take on difficult jobs and they have a lot of endurance. Moreover, even in the most traumatic circumstances they can appear calm, cool, and collected.

Virgos may actually be quite anxious or self-conscious underneath their calm exteriors, but they maintain good poker faces, so others would never guess that they are suffering.

Strangely enough, Virgos tend to be better at dealing with major problems and hardships than the minor irritations and setbacks of daily life because the intense focus required during a serious crisis prevents them from dwelling on negative or anxious thoughts.

Frugal

Typical Virgos are good with money. The negative manifestation of this trait is a tendency toward miserliness. However, most Virgos will engage in a more positive frugality, making smart financial choices and refraining from squandering their money on stupid, wasteful, or pointless things.

Virgos rarely make frivolous expenditures, unless their ascendants are in a more extravagant signs such as Gemini, Leo, Libra, Sagittarius, or Aquarius. Purchases are usually well thought out rather than made on a whim because Virgos deal with stress by working on things, making things, organizing things, cleaning things, or analyzing things rather than shopping for things.

Virgos do not feel a need to show off, so they are not inclined to buy things just to impress others. They purchase only what they need rather than wasting their money on status symbols, and they favor items that will last over those that are trendy or flashy.

Most Virgos prefer not to engage in social activities that require throwing their money away with nothing to show for it. They would rather stay home reading a good book or watching a favorite show with a few friends or a partner than go out on the town.

Virgos do not understand people who are careless with their cash. They appreciate common sense and take a negative view of those who squander their money on a good time and then go around borrowing from others. Although Virgos are willing to help unfortunates who are broke due to bad luck, they have no sympathy for people who are the authors of their own misfortunes.

Fussy

Virgos have a reputation for being fussy because they have a strong need to keep things a certain way. This fussiness arises not from a domineering nature, but instead from a need to control their environments as much as possible to reduce their anxiety. Their homes, belongings, and routines tend to be very well-organized, and they find it upsetting when others leave things lying around all over the place or refuse to make plans in advance.

Some Virgos can become overly picky or even tyrannical about household issues, demanding that everyone organize and maintain things to their specifications. However, most will keep silent to keep the peace, quietly putting everything back in order each day. They may seethe internally or become distressed by the chaos, but they understand that their need for order is unusually intense and that they cannot expect everyone else to conform to their requirements.

Virgo fussiness also manifests as a tendency toward perfectionism. Virgos take pride in everything they do. They will not do something unless they plan to do it well, and that means attending to all the fine details that make the difference between an exceptional job and an adequate one. As a result, they can appear nitpicky when working on projects with others. Their standards tend to be higher, and this can be off-putting to those who are happy to turn in substandard work just to be done with things.

Many Virgos are also fussy about food, eating sparingly or confining themselves to a limited range of options. Food sensitivities or aversions often prevent them from eating as much junk food as those of other signs, so they are more likely to stay relatively lean and fit throughout their lives, unless their ascendants are in more decadent, self-indulgent signs such as Taurus, Leo, Sagittarius, or Pisces.

Hardworking

Virgos are among the most hardworking signs of the zodiac. They do not expect to have things handed to them; Instead, they are willing to do their fair share (or more than their fair share) to get what they need or want.

Virgos gain great satisfaction from a job well done. They put in a thorough, conscientious effort with every project they undertake, and they do not require lavish praise or recognition. Humble by nature, they work hard to produce exceptional things or to help others without needing to have their egos stroked (unless their ascendants are in more attention-seeking signs).

Many Virgos are drawn to demanding professions that provide opportunities to help people or animals, or to improve the natural environment. They have a need to be needed and to serve meaningful causes, so many are drawn to volunteer work as well.

Health-conscious

Virgos are very health-conscious. The positive manifestation of this trait is a tendency to be active, which improves their mental health in addition to providing physical health benefits. Virgos are also less likely than those of other signs to overeat or abuse substances, unless other elements in their natal zodiacs incline them toward sensation seeking (for example, Leo or Sagittarius rising) or escapism (a Pisces ascendant). Virgos tend to stay fit well into old age, so many look far younger than their years.

Virgos like to stay up-to-date with the newest research on fitness and nutrition. Most have an interest in all health-related topics, especially diet and exercise routines. They tend to be careful about what they eat and favor natural or whole foods over heavily processed options. Many also take supplements or herbal remedies.

Although health-consciousness brings many benefits, some Virgos take this trait to the extreme, succumbing to hypochondria. Hypochondriacal Virgos worry about even the most minor symptoms, obsessively searching for medical information online and becoming extremely anxious about the possibility that there might be something terribly wrong with them. Fortunately, most Virgos manage to keep this in check, though the tendency to obsess over symptoms usually increases in times of stress.

Helpful

Virgos are happiest when helping others. Some are inclined to befriend or even marry people with mental or physical health problems because they are drawn to those who need them. Others gravitate to animal rescue work, environmental activities, or other charitable pursuits. Typical Virgos have a strong desire to serve a good cause, and they can work very hard on behalf of worthy objectives even when the rewards are minimal to nonexistent.

Virgos have a strong need to be needed, along with a talent for healing the sick and providing practical advice and assistance. Their advice is usually worth following because it tends to be based on a thoughtful analysis of the benefits and drawbacks associated with a potential course of action rather than a knee-jerk emotional reaction.

Because they have such a strong drive to help, Virgos may be drawn to service professions such as medicine, rescue work, rehabilitative work, or work with animals. They also provide practical assistance to friends in need. Although Virgos are not usually the best choice for an emotional discussion, they are quick to offer tangible assistance, such as helping a friend move, taking care of a sick companion, or doing what needs to be done to help someone escape or overcome a bad situation.

Humble

Typical Virgos are not at all egotistical. Instead, they tend to deflect praise and allow others to take credit. Their self-esteem comes from within and from what they do rather than what others say about them, so they do not go around fishing for compliments or demanding attention and recognition.

Modest by nature, most Virgos dislike flashy clothing and avoid doing things that would draw attention. They hate being the center of attention and would rather let others hog the spotlight while they stay quietly in the background.

Some Virgos take humility to the extreme, refusing to put themselves forward or demand the recognition they are due. They are often the ones who do more work on a project than other team members or come up with good ideas for which others take credit.

Virgos can suffer from low self-esteem because they tend to focus on what they would like to improve about themselves or the ways they have fallen short of their own high standards rather than their many good qualities and achievements. Developing self-esteem, self-love, and self-compassion can be major challenges for this sign.

Intellectual

Virgos love to learn new things and they seek intellectual stimulation through intelligent conversation or solo pursuits such as reading non-fiction or complicated fiction, doing crossword puzzles, learning to play musical instruments, or playing games that require strategy or analysis.

Virgos quickly grow bored with people who are content to make small talk or chatter about frivolous things. They are interested in deeper topics and they engage with others to exchange ideas rather than simply to socialize, so they would rather be alone than participate in conversations that do not interest them.

Introverted

Virgos tend to be introverted unless their ascendants are in more outgoing signs such as Aries, Gemini, Leo, Libra, Sagittarius, or Aquarius. They enjoy spending time on their own and they need this time to recharge their social batteries. Time alone out in nature, exercising, and/or reading are particularly restorative for Virgos.

Typical Virgos do not seek out big parties or nightclubs. They would rather socialize around activities (a hike, a game night, sports, crafts, a building project, etc.), and they prefer small groups of friends or one-on-one social interaction to large gatherings.

Because Virgos do not have a strong need to socialize, they can be selective about their companions, choosing people who genuinely interest them. Virgos would rather be alone than settle for people who do not meet their requirements.

Logical

The Virgo nature is more akin to that of Spock than Kirk in the Star Trek series. Virgos think things through and make rational decisions rather than acting on gut feelings. They take the time to weigh all possible outcomes and the risks and benefits of decisions rather than leaping blindly into something new.

Virgos are bewildered by those who behave irrationally. They do not understand why some people are not persuaded by evidence, instead forming opinions and choosing ideologies based on feelings.

Virgos tend to make good decisions and select the right course of action in a crisis because they make rational choices. They are also good at guiding others toward sensible options, preventing friends and family members from making terrible mistakes.

Because they tend to make their decisions and arguments based on logic rather than gut feelings or faith, more emotional types may perceive Virgos as cold. However, Virgos are capable of great compassion, but they can suppress their feelings when contemplating decisions so that they err on the side of practicality.

Patient

Virgos are very patient. While others act on careless impulses, Virgos take the time required to assess consequences and alternative options before acting.

Because Virgos are so patient and sensible, most are immune to get-rich-quick schemes and belief in magic bullets for problems such as health issues, relationship troubles, and weight loss. Instead, they are willing to do the hard work and put in the time required to achieve things.

Virgos also tend to be patient with others. They are sympathetic toward those who require a slower pace and not inclined to become pushy or irritable with more ponderous individuals. Virgos understand that they will not get the results they want by applying pressure;

instead, they wait patiently for others to catch up physically or intellectually.

Perfectionistic

Virgos are perfectionists in all they do. Although this trait enables them to produce superior work, it has a dark side.

Virgos hold themselves to impossibly high standards and can become very self-critical or even depressed if they fail to live up to their unreasonably high expectations.

Negative Virgos may also become very critical of others, pointing out their shortfalls and nitpicking their work. If this becomes a habit, they can destroy the self-esteem of their children and partners, anger coworkers, and drive friends and lovers away. However, most Virgos focus more on their own imperfections or flaws (often minor or even imagined) rather than those of others.

There is an old saying that Virgos should heed: "Do not let the perfect become the enemy of the good." When Virgos let their perfectionistic tendencies get the better of them, nothing can ever be finished because nothing is ever good enough, so they may never release that story or piece of art or complete that household project or anything else they attempt. A big challenge for Virgos is determining when something is good enough and learning to be satisfied with that.

Practical

Like the other earth signs, Taurus and Capricorn, Virgos are practical by nature. They make pragmatic choices such as saving money rather than blowing it on impulse purchases and they rarely endanger their health and safety with reckless choices. If Virgos do engage in dangerous sports, they are very safety conscious, carefully checking all their gear and supplies and doing everything they can to manage and mitigate the risk.

Typical Virgos will purchase insurance, get regular medical checkups, have emergency supplies on hand, and create plans for dealing with various disaster scenarios, and they do not understand those who fail to prepare for difficult situations.

Because they are so practical, Virgos are more interested in action than theory. If new knowledge becomes available, they want to know how it can be applied to make the world a better place, or at least improve some small aspect of it.

Virgos are doers who want to make a tangible difference in the world. Others may sit around and speculate as to how things could be made better, but Virgos are interested in action, so they will only participate in groups whose talk leads to realistic plans.

Reliable

Typical Virgos are very reliable. They show up on time and keep their promises and commitments, and they are dependable workers who do not take time off unless they are seriously ill, badly injured, or dealing with a major crisis. Virgos are more likely to soldier on through a major illness or significant psychological distress than take to their beds at the first sniffle or sign of anxiety or sadness.

Virgos place a high value on reliability in others as well. The quickest ways to lose their respect are to break promises, alter plans at the last minute, or fail to show up for prearranged meetings. Virgos need to feel that they can trust others in their life; anyone they cannot count on will soon be jettisoned in favor of more dependable companions.

Skeptical

Because they are logical thinkers, Virgos tend to be skeptical. They will not take something on pure faith; those who seek to convince them must provide compelling evidence, and the more fantastical the claim, the better the evidence needs to be.

Virgos are less likely than those of other signs to fall for scams or join cults. Their initial reflex, particularly when hearing something that sounds too good to be true, is to doubt the claims and conduct independent research. Virgos are willing to change their beliefs, but they will only do so if there is good evidence supporting the alternative.

Talented

Most Virgos have many talents. They are not necessarily born with these aptitudes, but because they are willing to work hard at anything that interests them and put in the hours required to master things, they tend to develop superior skills.

Typical areas of talent for Virgos include linguistics, mathematics, nutrition, medicine (including alternative or complementary therapies), research, writing, editing, design, and practical crafts. However, Virgos will take the time to become experts at anything that interests them, regardless of whether they have any innate talent.

The Atypical Virgo

The sun sign is not the only element that influences personality. Aspects and planetary placements, particularly the moon sign and rising sign (ascendant), are also important. For example, a Virgo with Sagittarius rising will be more laid back, extroverted, and careless, and with Leo rising, a Virgo will be less cautious and sensible and more optimistic, attention-seeking, and romantic. Taurus rising will enhance the pragmatic, down-to-earth side of Virgo, while an Aquarius ascendant brings out the intellectual, experimental side at the expense of practicality.

There are many websites that offer free chart calculation to determine your other planetary placements and aspects. Learning these other planetary placements is recommended, as it provides a more comprehensive personality profile.

See Appendix 2 for information about other astrological influences on personality.

Chapter 2: Virgo Love and Friendship Style

Virgos are diplomatic, undemanding, and thoughtful companions who value intelligence above style and stability over intensity in romantic relationships and friendships. They do best with calm, practical, reasonable companions who have a passion for learning and intellectual development.

Selective

Virgos are very choosy when it comes to friends and lovers—they won't hang around with just anyone.

Virgos do fall in love, but it takes a very special person to win them over because they are independent by nature and afraid of being hurt. They hate to be vulnerable to others and love is the greatest vulnerability, so they do not fall in love easily and they are very selective.

Some Virgos are voluntarily single due to emotional caution or because they would rather be on their own than settle for a badly flawed relationship. They also tend to be fastidious, and they have difficulty tolerating people who are careless about cleanliness and personal hygiene.

Virgos require a strong base of shared interests to maintain close relationships. Most are interested in fitness, health, or nutrition, and they use this knowledge to positively influence the habits of those around them. Virgos do best with friends and lovers who share their fitness and health pursuits.

Practical

Ideal companions for Virgos are those who appreciate love shown through considerate and helpful actions rather than romantic words and gestures or emotionally charged discussions about feelings. Typical

Virgos are happy to receive useful gifts rather than showy things that have no practical value, and they demonstrate their love with practical gifts and gestures as well.

Virgos are quick to assist friends in need when they require practical help. Although they have trouble dealing with emotional outpourings and finding the right words to provide comfort, Virgos are very good at helping friends and lovers in tangible ways that involve physically doing something for the other person.

Inquisitive

Virgos have a powerful intellectual curiosity about other people, and this intense focus is sometimes mistaken for romantic interest. Analytical and intrigued by human nature, Virgos want to learn what makes their friends and lovers tick.

Typical Virgos like to know how things work and how to do things, so they spend much of their free time researching topics of interest. They appreciate companions who are similarly interested in learning new things and those who have useful knowledge to impart.

Virgos are usually drawn to people by intellectual curiosity rather than for shallower reasons. Because they need intellectual stimulation, they will quickly grow bored in the company of those who make small talk rather than speaking of serious, important things.

Virgos are attracted by brilliant minds rather than surface charm and slick banter, so they are less likely to be taken in by sociopaths who win others over with a combination of charisma and flattery.

Virgos can be dazzled by beauty like everyone else. However, they are quick to get over their infatuation if the beautiful individual is not intellectually dazzling as well.

Reasonable

Virgos are reasonable companions, not prone to creating emotional drama or picking fights. Classy and self-controlled by nature, Virgos are unlikely to make ugly scenes in public. Most are low-maintenance partners and friends who do not make excessive demands on others (in fact, they are unlikely to ask for help even when they desperately need it).

Common sense, modesty, and diplomacy enable Virgos to get along well with most people, though they may prefer the company of animals to that of most people unless their ascendants are in more outgoing fire or air signs.

Even atypically extroverted Virgos will usually hang back in social situations while they assess others they have just met because they do not like to put themselves forward until they know what sort of people they are dealing with. They prefer not to engage with those who are unreasonable, unreliable, or unpredictable, so they spend some time observing new prospects before establishing a true friendship or making or responding to romantic overtures.

Active

Unless they have more outgoing ascendants, Virgos need to spend time alone pursing their own activities. When they do socialize, they prefer to do something intellectually or physically active with their companions.

Virgos like to be exercising either their bodies or their minds at all times, and they will quickly grow restless when not on the move mentally or physically. They are rarely happy with unmotivated individuals. Instead, they seek companions who are as active and motivated as they are.

Strong in Adversity

Virgos are wonderful to have around when a friend, family member, or partner is in need because they will do what is necessary to ensure that any sick or vulnerable person is well taken care of. Virgos are often at their best when situations or other people are at their worst, providing tangible support and applying common sense to solve problems and relieve the distress of friends and partners.

Although they project a calm demeanor even in difficult situations, Virgos are natural worriers. Ideal companions are those who encourage them to share their anxieties and help them put these fears and obsessive thoughts into perspective so that they do not become overwhelming.

Emotionally Reserved

Virgos are slow to trust and warm up to new people, and they will rarely engage in spontaneous hugging and other physical demonstrations of affection until they know someone very well. Even then, such demonstrations may not be frequent (at least in public). However, when Virgos do show physical affection, companions can be sure that it is a genuine expression of friendship or love rather than a meaningless gesture offered to anyone.

Virgo emotional detachment and repression of feelings usually keep fights and destructive impulses to a minimum (the exception to this rule is a Virgo with a more passionate rising sign). However, this impressive self-control and tendency to think rather than feel things out can make Virgos appear uncaring, and this perception is exacerbated by the Virgo ability to walk away from relationships suddenly without looking back.

Because they tend not to show emotions or express their feelings openly, when Virgos are unhappy in a situation, their partners may not realize that there is a problem until it is too late. Virgos disentangle from people relatively easily and with as little fuss as possible, making the decision to go based on a rational analysis of the situation rather than emotion and slipping away quietly to avoid emotional drama whenever possible.

Chapter 3: Virgo Compatibility with Other Sun Signs

Note: There is more to astrological compatibility than sun signs alone. Other elements in a person's natal zodiac also play a role. Ascendants (rising signs), moon signs, and other planetary placements and aspects also shape personality and affect compatibility. For example, a Virgo with Leo rising will be more extroverted, emotionally demonstrative, and attention-seeking than a typical Virgo, and an Aquarius with Taurus rising or the moon in Scorpio will be more compatible with Virgo than a typical Aquarius. For more information on other natal chart elements, see Appendix 2.

Virgo + Aries

This is among the most challenging combinations for both signs. Virgo caution and practicality clashes with Aries recklessness; Virgo's tendency to criticize triggers the infamous Aries rebelliousness; and the Aries tendency toward exuberant (and sometimes inappropriate) public behavior can distress modest, quiet Virgo. Overall, these two signs are so drastically different from one another that it is difficult for them to get along or see eye to eye on anything unless their ascendants and moon signs are more compatible.

Virgo tends to be analytical and pragmatic while Aries is restless and impulsive. Aries may grow impatient with Virgo's tendency to think things through carefully and weigh all the pros and cons of any decision before making it, while Virgo will be distressed by the Arian tendency to throw caution to the winds. Lifestyle preferences may also be a source of friction, as Virgo is drawn to the natural world, solitary pursuits, and the inner world of the mind, whereas the typical Aries wants more social experiences.

Virgo and Aries may find some common ground based on Virgo's desire to stay active, which is compatible with the Aries need for action. If a Virgo enjoys hiking or athletic pursuits, these two can share outdoor adventures, and if the Aries social drive leads to intellectually stimulating interactions, Virgo will want to participate.

In a best-case scenario, these two will open one another's minds to new ideas and ways of living, cultivating a balance of their best traits while minimizing their less appealing attributes. In a worst-case scenario, Aries will find Virgo cold and unknowable while Virgo finds Aries selfish and irritating.

The most significant problem with the Aries-Virgo match is that both will want to do things their own way and neither is likely to give in, which can make living together stressful (unless one or both individuals have more compromising ascendants). On the other hand, Virgo's lack of jealousy allows Aries more personal freedom than many other signs will comfortably grant their partners, so this pairing does have some potential if other elements in their natal zodiacs are more compatible.

Virgo + Taurus

This is often a good combination. Both signs tend to be reliable and trustworthy (unless other elements in their natal zodiacs incline them toward uncharacteristic irresponsibility), so they can count on one another, even when times are hard. Taurus and Virgo also have complementary traits that enhance their compatibility. Taurus provides the stability and calmness that anxious Virgo needs while Virgo's greater flexibility and open-mindedness have a beneficial effect on Taurus, making conversations intellectually stimulating and reducing the likelihood that the relationship will grow boring.

There is a lot of stability and practicality in this pairing, as well as a high likelihood of shared interests. Both individuals are drawn to the natural world, so they are likely to enjoy outdoor pursuits (though nothing too reckless). Both will probably also enjoy home-based projects such as building things for the house or creating a garden. And although there probably will not be much spontaneity with this match, neither individual is likely to be bothered by this as both are far too sensible to go off in search of danger (unless their ascendants are in fire signs).

One potential problem with this combination is that Virgo might not be affectionate enough for Taurus in a romantic pairing, though Taurus has a better chance than most of encouraging Virgo to abandon inhibitions.

Virgo tends to show love by doing helpful things for others or buying them practical gifts rather than with splashy romantic gestures, and Taurus will appreciate these useful actions and items, responding in kind. Overall, this tends to be a good pairing for friendship or romance unless other elements in their natal zodiacs are highly unfavorable.

Virgo + Gemini

Although this is an intellectually stimulating combination, there is likely to be a lot of friction between these two. Virgo may find Gemini too inconsistent and unreliable, while Gemini finds Virgo overly cautious or critical. On the other hand, both signs are cerebral and analytical by nature, so they can have plenty of fascinating conversations and learn a lot from one another. If their ascendants and moon signs are compatible, this can be an interesting match.

Virgo and Gemini both crave food for thought and they can enjoy a wonderful intellectual rapport, but Virgos are more interested in how ideas can be practically applied, whereas Geminis entertain ideas for their own sake. Geminis tend to skip from one thing to the next without delving deeply into anything, while Virgos are inclined to obsessively learn all they can about particular topics. These complementary learning styles can be beneficial, if Gemini introduces Virgo to a breadth of ideas and interests and Virgo helps Gemini develop a more in-depth knowledge and understanding of things.

An additional point in favor of this relationship is that both signs tend to be emotionally detached, so neither will be bothered by this trait in the other. However, because neither sign is prone to the emotional intensity that exerts a tight hold, one or the other may wander off in search of new connections if they find the relationship difficult or not entirely fulfilling.

Living together day to day can be a challenge for this pair, as they tend to like different activities and have different lifestyle preferences. The typical Virgo is a homebody, preferring spend time with a good book, visit with a small number of close friends, work on personal projects, tend a garden, or go for a hike, while the typical Gemini wants to get out and mingle with a broad array of people and try a variety of new activities. Geminis also tend to have a greater interest in culture, whereas Virgos are more drawn to the natural world, and Virgos thrive on routine and security, while Geminis grow restless or anxious if things get too settled and predictable.

One particularly serious problem with this pairing is that Gemini and Virgo have different ways of dealing with the practical aspects of life. Virgos keep their commitments and are very judgmental of those who do not, while Geminis tend to show up late (if at all), and although they are generous with their time and money, they are not particularly reliable unless their ascendants incline them toward greater conscientiousness. They can be generous when helping a friend in need, but they cannot always be counted on for less urgent commitments. Virgo can also be distressed by the infamous Gemini impracticality and poor money management skills, and will usually respond by nagging and criticizing, which will drive Gemini crazy (or out the door).

Virgo and Gemini are very different people unless their ascendants bring their temperaments into better alignment, so they may fail to appreciate one another's better qualities and become overly fixated on what they dislike in each other. In a worst-case scenario, Virgo will view Gemini as immature, superficial, and unreliable, while Gemini finds Virgo fussy, judgmental, and repressive. In a best-case scenario, these two will enjoy their strong intellectual connection and have their lifestyle needs met by engaging in outside interests while remaining loyal to one another in the ways that count. A positive aspect of this pairing is that neither sign is inclined to be jealous or possessive, so they can allow one another the freedom to engage in activities outside the primary relationship.

Virgo + Cancer

Although Virgo might not be sufficiently affectionate or demonstrative for Cancer's taste, in most ways this is a compatible match. Both signs tend to be practical, reliable, and concerned with health and domestic issues, and both are helpful and self-sacrificing by nature, which means that they are unlikely to abandon one another in times of need. Virgo and Cancer can create a comfortable home together, establish a mutually supportive friendship, or run a successful business.

Cancer and Virgo have some complementary traits that increase their overall compatibility. For example, Virgos have a strong need to control their environments, whereas Cancers tend to be less fussy and more flexible about their homes and workplaces. This means that Cancers often let Virgos organize shared homes to suit their own preferences (which is critical to Virgo happiness). Also, Virgos tend to be stoic in the face of hardship or loss, so they can support Cancers through difficult or unpleasant situations. In addition, neither is inclined to take off when things get rough, so these two can form a good support system for one another. Both also tend to be worriers, so they are usually sympathetic and willing to provide reassurance, as needed.

Despite its many positive attributes, the Cancer-Virgo match is not without challenges. The most significant problem with this pairing is that Cancers tend to experience the world through their emotions and Virgos through their intellects. Virgos have difficulty relating to Cancerian feelings; a criticism Virgo considers insignificant can be devastating for Cancer, so there is a risk that Virgo will inflict deep wounds without realizing it. In such cases, Cancer may perceive Virgo as cold and unfeeling, while Virgo thinks Cancer is being oversensitive, and both are inclined to be critical, which can make matters worse. On the other hand, Virgos tend to be considerate and have good self-restraint, so they can learn to tread cautiously around Cancerian feelings.

In a best-case scenario, these two will have positive effects on one another, with Cancer encouraging Virgo to warm up and explore the emotional side of life, and Virgo helping Cancer develop some self-protective emotional detachment. Each can soothe the other's anxieties, Virgo by helping Cancer see that things are not as bad as they seem, and Cancer by compromising and accommodating Virgo's need to maintain things in certain ways. However, for the relationship to succeed, these two will have to develop a better understanding of the different ways in which each experiences the world so that they can be more attuned to each other's feelings and needs.

Despite their differences in perception, Cancer and Virgo usually have plenty in common when it comes to lifestyle preferences. They are often drawn to the natural world of quiet green spaces and both need to establish solid incomes and stable home bases to feel secure. Neither is inclined toward recklessness unless they have their ascendants in Scorpio or one of the fire signs (Aries, Leo, or Sagittarius), so they are less likely to destroy one another financially or put their lives at risk unnecessarily. Both typically prefer the company of close friends and family to attending large gatherings as they tend to be somewhat shy around new people (unless their ascendants are in more gregarious signs). They also share a penchant for practical crafts, which can form the basis for mutual interests in making or building things. In addition, Cancers are rarely pushy and Virgos are not inclined to pick fights, so although the relationship may lack excitement, it is likely to be supportive, harmonious, and mutually fulfilling.

Virgo + Leo

This match can be challenging because these two signs have such different ways of relating to the world. Leo may find Virgo too private and cautious, and Virgo will probably find Leo too desperate for praise and attention. Virgo is intellectually focused and somewhat aloof, which can be upsetting for passionate, affectionate Leo. And Leo tends to be noisy, boisterous, and prone to risk taking, which can be stressful for quiet, careful Virgo.

One of the most significant difficulties with this pairing is that Leo is proud and sensitive to criticism while Virgo is contemptuous of large egos and compelled to deflate them. Leos may suffer devastating blows to their self-esteem when Virgos make unflattering judgments (what Virgo considers constructive criticism is likely to be perceived as a personal attack by Leo). Leos are also likely to find emotionally reserved Virgos insufficiently demonstrative and romantic. To make matters worse, the typical Leo is more sociable than the typical Virgo and is unlikely to understand Virgo's need for time alone (Leo may even take this as a personal rejection). In a romantic relationship, Virgo will probably find Leo's need for attention and adoration perplexing and irritating, and Leo may find Virgo cold or overly cautious.

The primary reason why Virgos need solitary time or prefer to spend time with small groups of friends rather than a big crowd is that they are prone to anxiety and thrive in calm environments. Typical Leos, by contrast, are energized by noisy, action-packed environments, so these two may disagree about social activities.

Another problem with this pairing is that Leos tend to be emotionally expressive and quick to anger (though also quick to forgive), while Virgos are inclined to avoid conflict (and those who provoke it). This clash of styles can leave Virgo in a chronic state of distress, and Virgo is quick to leave (or at least retreat from) strife-ridden situations.

An additional difference between these two is that Leos tend to show their love with grand romantic words and gestures, whereas Virgos typically do so with considerate practical actions and useful gifts. In a positive relationship, this could be beneficial, as both will enjoy doing things for each other. However, in a negative relationship, Leo may find Virgo's gifts boring and unromantic, while Virgo finds Leo's presents unnecessarily expensive and useless (a typical Leo is more likely to appreciate gifts of fine food, expensive alcoholic beverages, or luxury items, while a typical Virgo would rather give or receive a practical gift).

The success of this relationship will probably depend Virgo's willingness to be more careful with Leo's delicate pride and more overtly affectionate, and Leo's ability to rein in the spending and grow a thicker skin when it comes to taking criticism. In a best-case scenario, Leo will help Virgo lighten up and become less anxious and more sociable, and Virgo will help Leo develop the self-restraint and diligence necessary to do something productive with Leo's many creative and potentially lucrative ideas.

Virgo and Leo often share some common ground in the form of interests and activities that may increase the likelihood of relationship success. Leos tend to be creative and most Virgos enjoy practical crafts or building things, so these two may engage in creative, constructive pursuits together. Many Virgos also like home-based activities such as gardening and cooking nutritious food, and Leos tend to have green thumbs and a flare for cooking and baking as well (though they are more inclined to focus on decadent treats than the health-promoting meals Virgos favor). Both signs like to be active, so they may also share an interest in sports or rugged outdoor hobbies. In addition, health-conscious Virgos tend to stay in relatively good shape, which is important to appearance-conscious Leos. If these two have shared interests and other elements in their natal zodiacs are more compatible, this match has potential.

Virgo + Virgo

This tends to be an intellectually stimulating and stable match, though it may not be the most exciting pairing in a romantic relationship. Two Virgos can stir one another up intellectually, but they are less likely to stimulate passion in each other unless other factors in their natal zodiacs create more friction. However, compatibility tends to be high with this match, and a relationship between two Virgos that looks boring to more gregarious types is unlikely to be boring for the Virgos because they will have so many fascinating conversations.

Virgos tend to be pragmatic and sensible, and this is reflected in their approach to love and friendship. They are more inclined to show their love by giving useful gifts or taking on unpleasant errands or chores to spare their partners, family members, or friends the hassle than with extravagant presents or splashy romantic gestures. Virgos are not inclined toward public displays of affection, though they are happy to snuggle up at home with a trusted companion.

A pair of Virgos will probably lead an active life together, so this match can have a health-promoting effect. Virgos like to keep fit and usually exercise regularly to burn off their nervous energy. Although most do not enjoy noisy, rambunctious gatherings, typical Virgos do like getting out for physical pursuits in nature such as walking, hiking, or sports, or going to the gym. The majority also share an interest in healthy eating, so they have a higher-than-average likelihood of looking and feeling good even in their later years.

In most cases there is not too much for two Virgos to fight about. Both tend to be somewhat introverted and to prefer spending time alone with their partners or in smaller gatherings of well-known friends to big, noisy events. Both tend to be good with money and not prone to taking ill-advised risks that endanger their finances or their health. However, there is one potential problem with this pairing.

Virgos have very strong preferences regarding their home environments. If these preferences line up well, the relationship is likely to be harmonious. On the other hand, if there are significant differences in the way these two individuals want to decorate and organize their home, it will be difficult for either of them to give in because controlling their environments is very important to Virgos. However, there is a better-than-average likelihood that preferences will line up reasonably well when two Virgos get together.

Virgo + Libra

These two signs usually get along reasonably well. Both tend to be fastidious and intellectually focused. Also, Virgo is not particularly possessive and has a higher tolerance for Libra's flirting than those of many other signs, and Libra can tolerate Virgo's fussiness because Libras are not inclined to quibble over details, so they tend to let Virgos have their way over the small issues. Both signs tend to be diplomatic and they share an intense dislike of conflict, which reduces the likelihood of fights. However, there are significant differences in lifestyle preferences and the ways in which these two signs relate to the world that may create problems.

Libras tend to be highly sociable. They enjoy mixing with others and sharing ideas. Although Virgos also seek the intellectual stimulation of discussion and debate, they are quick to tire of the endless rounds of socializing that Libras usually prefer and have little patience for gatherings where small talk is the norm. A typical Libra could happily spend every night at a party or a pub, or in some other venue with friends and plenty of new people to mix things up. A typical Virgo, on the other hand, needs plenty of time alone to recharge and prefers smaller gatherings of long-time companions to a raucous crowd. Social orientations will be brought into better alignment if the Libra has a more introverted rising sign or the Virgo has a more gregarious ascendant.

Libras are also romantic idealists, which can clash with Virgo's tendency toward realism (sensible Virgo may burst Libra's bubbles of optimism from time to time). Another potential source of conflict between these two signs is that Libra is more likely to be open-minded and non-judgemental, while Virgo tends to be skeptical and analytical. Also, Libras crave flattery and crumble under criticism, and Virgos can be quite direct (they are not inclined to stroke egos). This can lead to a situation where Libra is easily charmed by someone else who is more complimentary, or Virgo leaves in search of someone who requires less bolstering.

Another problem with this pairing is that Libra likes to spend money on a good time (and on looking good), while Virgo tends to be more practical and cautious with money. In a worst-case scenario, Virgo will find Libra shallow, frivolous, and self-indulgent, while Libra finds Virgo uptight and repressive. However, in a best-case scenario, Libra will adopt some of Virgo's common sense, and Virgo's hidden sensuality will be brought to the surface by Libra's warm, affectionate nature. This pair will always have lots of interesting things to talk about and they will probably find one another's minds fascinating, even if living together requires a significant amount of compromise.

Virgo + Scorpio

This is a good combination for friendship and romance. Virgos and Scorpios have a lot in common. They share a number of traits, including strong work ethics, powerful minds, high-intensity inner lives, a tendency to hide their feelings, independent natures, and the need to spend time on solitary pursuits. A relationship between these two may get off to a slow start because these signs are wary and even somewhat distrustful, but once it gets going, this match can be very deep and stable.

One potential problem with this pairing is that Scorpio may crave more passion in a romantic relationship or become insecure if Virgo's emotional reserve is mistaken for lack of interest. Another problem area may be lack of communication. Scorpio is slow to trust and tends to be secretive, and Virgo is restrained by nature, making this sign difficult to know and understand. As a result, these two may have trouble opening up and sharing their true feelings with one another. On the other hand, Scorpio's possessiveness will make Virgo feel more secure about the relationship, and Virgo's intellectual strength will maintain Scorpio's interest.

Despite a few minor issues, this pairing has a lot going for it. Both signs favor depth over surface charm, preferring to discuss the profound issues in life and abhorring small talk. These two are also likely to match well in terms of lifestyle preferences. Both tend toward introversion, and although they do socialize, they also need plenty of time on their own to pursue personal interests and recharge their batteries. When this pair go out into the world together, Virgo is less likely to set off the infamous Scorpio jealousy by playing emotional games or flirting with anyone (Virgos rarely flirt with people they do not intend to actively pursue).

One significant difference between these two signs is that Scorpios are natural risk takers while Virgos tend to be cautious, testing the waters before jumping in. Each approach is better suited to particular situations, so ideally these two will have positive effects on one another, with Scorpio encouraging Virgo to take calculated risks and Virgo putting the brakes on some of Scorpio's more foolhardy impulses. Another difference between these two is that Scorpios do not mind getting their hands dirty, whereas typical Virgos hate to do this in both the metaphorical and real senses. This is another area in which these two can have a positive influence on each other, with Scorpio helping Virgo overcome this contamination phobia and Virgo encouraging Scorpio to develop a little more caution when necessary.

Virgo + Sagittarius

This is a very difficult combination unless other elements in their natal zodiacs are far more compatible. While this pairing is intellectually stimulating, and sensation-seeking Sagittarius can encourage cautious Virgo to open up and try new things, there is not much stability with this match unless these two have their ascendants in more commitment-oriented signs such as Taurus, Cancer, Leo, Scorpio, or Capricorn. In a worst-case scenario, Virgo will find Sagittarius irresponsible and unreliable, and Sagittarius will find Virgo too cautious and serious. These two will probably irritate one another in a deeper relationship, though in a casual acquaintanceship they can share interesting ideas.

Virgo and Sagittarius have very different needs and different ideas about what constitutes a good life. If they decide to live together, they will probably have to compromise on many lifestyle issues. Sagittarians tend to be gregarious and extroverted. They need to get out and meet new people on a regular basis and will even spend time with people they do not respect or even like if they find them interesting. Virgos, by contrast, prefer to cultivate a smaller number of close friendships with people they can trust, and to spend time with these close companions in less boisterous venues. One potential compromise for these two is to combine socializing with outdoor pursuits such as hiking or sports so that the Sagittarian needs to move and interact and the Virgo requirements for physical activity and a peaceful setting can be met simultaneously.

On the plus side, Sagittarians and Virgos do have some complementary traits that allow them to either compensate for or complete one another. Sagittarians are big-picture people, whereas Virgos are detail-oriented. This can be helpful if these two start a business together because Sagittarius can handle the promotional and strategy aspects while Virgo tackles issues surrounding the development and delivery of a high-quality product or service.

Another complementary trait set (or point of contention) with this pair is Virgo cleanliness versus Sagittarian sloppiness. Although cleanliness is considered a virtue, Virgos can take it so far that it becomes a vice. Typical Sagittarians, on the other hand, are not domestic, germ-phobic, or house-proud, so their homes can become disaster areas. Ideally, these two will learn to compromise, with Virgo relaxing a bit on the issue of household hygiene and Sagittarius developing some better habits in this area.

One major problem with this pairing is that these signs have very different approaches to risk. Virgos will take risks, but only after carefully and thoroughly weighing the pros and cons so that they do not squander their resources or endanger their lives unnecessarily. Sagittarians prefer to trust in luck, leap without looking, and bet everything on a long shot. When unsure, Virgo will err on the side of caution, while Sagittarius will err on the side of risk. This difference could potentially lead to fights over a variety of issues, though squabbles about money are particularly likely. In a best-case scenario, Sagittarius will help Virgo lighten up and take a few reasonable chances, and Virgo will encourage Sagittarius to develop some much-needed restraint.

The trait that these two individuals have in common is the one that is most likely to drive them apart. Both tend to be blunt to a fault. In Virgo's case, this stems from a tendency to be critical, while Sagittarius is just generally insensitive (a Sagittarian will often blurt out anything that comes to mind without considering how it might affect the feelings of others). As a result, these two can do a lot of verbal damage to each another. In such cases, Virgo may leave in search of a more considerate and tactful partner, or Sagittarius may seek a less fussy and more lighthearted companion.

Overall, the Virgo-Sagittarius pairing will be very challenging unless their ascendants bring their temperaments into better alignment (for example, a Virgo with Aries, Libra, or Sagittarius rising is a better prospect for a Sagittarius, and if the Sagittarius has a Taurus, Virgo, or Capricorn ascendant, the rapport between these two will be much better). If other elements in their natal charts are more compatible, this can be an interesting and intellectually stimulating match.

Virgo + Capricorn

Virgo and Capricorn tend to be compatible. They have similar lifestyle preferences and goals, and they can count on one another to keep promises and finish what they start (unless their ascendants are in more flighty signs). This mutual reliability is good for any sort of relationship, whether it is a marriage, a friendship, or a business partnership.

Virgo and Capricorn tend to understand and respect one another. Both are conscientious, active, and health-conscious, which means that they are inclined to work hard, keep themselves in good shape, and build a secure and stable life together. These two can achieve a lot, regardless of what they set their minds to, and they respect each other's more underrated yet valuable traits such as diligence, pragmatism, and good work ethics. There is a risk that things will become routine with this relationship, but these two signs are more likely to appreciate stability than to find it boring.

Although the Virgo-Capricorn pairing has many strengths, because both signs tend to be emotionally cautious and slow to trust, confide in, and warm up to others, the relationship may be a slow starter, and even when it gets into full swing, it may not be particularly romantic. On an intimate level, there probably will not be much talk about feelings because neither of these signs likes emotional drama. As a result, they may avoid emotional discussions to the point where their connection is dry and intellectual. However, because neither sign tends to be needy or demanding, these two are unlikely to drain one another's energies.

Lack of demonstrativeness should not be a problem for this pair because neither seeks gushy public displays of affection. They are more inclined to show their love by purchasing gifts that support one another's hobbies, fitness activities, or home-based pursuits than to write mushy love letters or buy each other sentimental knick-knacks that have no practical value. Both signs appreciate these tangible demonstrations of love far more than empty words or romantic gestures.

Virgo + Aquarius

This can be a difficult combination. Although both individuals live largely in their minds and can develop a good intellectual rapport, it is unlikely that this relationship will go very deep unless their ascendants and moon signs bring their temperaments into better alignment.

Connecting emotionally can be challenging for this pair. Virgo is cautious and slow to trust, and Aquarius is not particularly sensitive. Unless other elements in their natal zodiacs create more warmth, these two individuals will be emotionally distant from each other and the relationship may lack affection. On the plus side, Virgo is less likely than those of many other signs to be jealous of Aquarius's outside activities and interests, and Aquarius will grant Virgo the freedom to pursue independent hobbies as well. However, these two may have difficulty living together because they have such different ways of interacting with the world.

Aquarian unpredictability will bother Virgo, and the typical Aquarius will not respect or even understand Virgo's need for consistency. Virgo craves security and can become very anxious in unstable situations, while Aquarius thrives on novelty and change. These conflicting tendencies may create a situation in which these two are often at cross-purposes, and both will have to do a lot of compromising to make their relationship work. In a worst-case scenario, they will drift apart due to different lifestyle preferences.

In addition to their sharp intellects, Virgo and Aquarius often share a desire to serve humanity in some way, so they can forge productive partnerships for charitable or political aims, but they are likely to irritate one another in day-to-day life. However, when they pair up, the connection tends to be intellectually stimulating and mind expanding, so this can be an interesting match, but it will have more potential if their ascendants bring their temperaments into better alignment (for example, a Virgo with Aries, Gemini, Libra, Sagittarius, or Aquarius rising is a better prospect for Aquarius, and an Aquarius with a Taurus, Cancer, Virgo, Scorpio, or Capricorn ascendant should be more compatible with Virgo).

Ideally, Virgo and Aquarius will have positive effects on one another, with Virgo steering Aquarius toward a healthier and more productive lifestyle and Aquarius introducing Virgo to new ideas and experiences. If these two establish a business partnership, the Aquarian visionary streak combined with the Virgo work ethic and achievement orientation could produce great things, provided these two are able to work together.

Virgo + Pisces

These two signs are often drawn to one another because each has what the other lacks, and the Virgo-Pisces match can be either sheer bliss or a source of perpetual aggravation. There is usually no middle ground with this pairing.

Pisces and Virgo are opposite signs of the zodiac and they have very different outlooks on life, but both are self-sacrificing on behalf of others, so they tend to be very generous toward those they care about. Pisceans are naturally innovative, creative, or spiritual, which are all good complements to Virgo's rational outlook, so these two individuals can open one another's minds to new perspectives. In addition, tolerant Pisces will probably let Virgo organize their home if these two live together, which is critical to Virgo's peace of mind. On the other hand, Piscean vagueness and escapist tendencies may irritate Virgo, and Virgo's exacting and critical nature could be stressful for Pisces.

In a best-case scenario, Virgo will provide the stability and healthy environment that Pisces needs, and Pisces will help Virgo open up and experience life more fully. Virgo will curb the worst Piscean excesses, and Pisces will help Virgo loosen up and be a little decadent from time to time. However, in a worst-case scenario, Virgo will find Pisces chaotic, unstable, and deceptive (or self-deceptive), while Pisces finds Virgo cold and cruel. Much will depend on other elements in their natal zodiacs.

Virgo and Pisces usually have some common ground in terms of lifestyle preferences. Both need plenty of time alone to refresh their minds, and both thrive in calm, peaceful environments. This means that they are less likely to clash over preferred activities and overall lifestyle choices. When they do come into conflict, it is more likely to occur because Pisces perceives Virgo as harsh and distant or Virgo feels that Pisces is being impractical and selfish.

Because these two individuals perceive and interact with the world in such different ways, it can be difficult for each to understand where the other is coming from, and as a result, they are likely to misinterpret one another's motives. To make this relationship work, these two will have to make an effort to understand one another's perspectives and avoid jumping to conclusions in response to statements or behaviors they do not understand. Communication and compromise will be the keys to success for this pairing. In addition, Virgo will need to develop a softer approach to criticism, and Pisces will have to work on becoming less emotionally reactive.

Chapter 4: Virgo Marriage

According to traditional astrologers, Virgos are most compatible with Taurus, Cancer, Virgo, Scorpio, and Capricorn, and least compatible with Aries, Gemini, Leo, Sagittarius, Aquarius, and Pisces. But what do the actual marriage and divorce statistics say?

Mathematician Gunter Sachs (1998) conducted a large-scale study of sun signs, encompassing nearly one million people in Switzerland, which found statistically significant results on a number of measures including marriage and divorce. Castille (2000) conducted a similar study in France using marriage statistics collected between 1976 and 1997, which included more than six million marriages.

Virgo sun sign pairings are ranked from most to least frequent on the pages that follow. *Indicates a statistically significant effect; in other words, the marriage rate was significantly higher or lower than would be expected by chance.

Virgo Men

Sachs Study

1. Virgo*

2. Scorpio

3. Taurus

4. Libra

5. Sagittarius

6. Capricorn (same as Cancer)

7. Cancer

8. Gemini

9. Leo

10. Aquarius

11. Pisces

12. Aries

Castille Study

1. Virgo*

2. Leo

3. Libra

4. Sagittarius

5. Scorpio

6. Cancer

7. Taurus

8. Capricorn

9. Gemini

10. Pisces

11. Aquarius

12. Aries*

Virgo Women

Sachs Study	Castille Study
1. Virgo*	1. Virgo*
2. Libra	2. Libra
3. Leo	3. Leo
4. Taurus	4. Taurus
5. Scorpio	5. Scorpio
6. Cancer	6. Cancer
7. Pisces	7. Pisces
8. Gemini	8. Gemini
9. Aries	9. Aries
10. Capricorn	10. Capricorn
11. Sagittarius	11. Sagittarius
12. Aquarius*	12. Aquarius*

Some Notes on Marriage Rates

In both Switzerland and France, Virgo men marry Virgo women more often than those of any other sign, and they marry Aries women least often (though this trend was only statistically significant in France). Virgo women were also most likely to marry Virgo men, but they were least likely to marry Aquarius men in both studies.

The common ground shared by two Virgos is probably what draws them together. Typical Virgos like intellectual pursuits, physical activities, charitable causes, or practical crafts, so they are likely to enjoy some of the same hobbies or interests.

The lifestyle preferences of two Virgos are likely to be compatible as well. Virgos are inclined toward introversion unless their ascendants are in fire or air signs, so they usually enjoy spending time on their own hobbies or with their partners or a couple of friends rather than seeking out big parties, nightclubs, and other crowded, noisy venues.

Most Virgos are also interested in doing things that will benefit the world, usually through sharing useful information or providing practical services, so two Virgos may bond over a shared cause.

An additional point of compatibility is their mutual hatred of emotional drama. Typical Virgos have little patience for anything shallow or frivolous. They rarely follow fads and trends, instead focusing on things of significance, and they value reliability and practicality above surface charm and style. They dislike splashy public displays of affection and emotional scenes, preferring to resolve conflicts in a rational, private manner, so they are unlikely to upset each other with embarrassing public meltdowns.

Given the common ground shared by two Virgos and their well-matched lifestyle and relational preferences, it is unsurprising that this pairing is the one most likely to make it to the altar.

Finding Aries at the bottom of the Virgo men's marriage list is also unsurprising, as it is challenging for these two signs to get along in day-to-day life unless other elements in their natal zodiacs are more compatible.

The directness (and, in some cases, pushiness) of Aries can aggravate Virgo, and Virgo cautiousness will irritate Aries as well.

Aries people tend to be emotionally demonstrative, feisty, impulsive, and reckless, whereas typical Virgos are diplomatic, thoughtful, emotionally reserved, and sensible, so these two are likely to clash on many different issues. However, their compatibility can be increased substantially if the Virgo an Aries, Gemini, Leo, Sagittarius, or Aquarius ascendant or moon sign, or the Aries has a Taurus, Cancer, Virgo, Scorpio, or Capricorn ascendant or moon sign.

Seeing Aquarius at the bottom of Virgo women's marriage list is also an expected finding because there is great potential for conflict between the two signs. Aquarius is among the least practical signs of the zodiac. Also, while both signs have a strong intellectual streak, typical Aquarians are extroverted and need to interact with groups of people on a regular basis, whereas Virgos tend to be lone wolves who prefer to spend time on their own or with their partners and close friends rather than in larger groups.

Mundane household issues can also be problematic for this pair. Virgos like to acquire only practical, useful objects and keep them well-organized, whereas Aquarians are more likely to collect an eclectic assortment of items, many of which do not have practical uses, and scatter them throughout the house. Virgos may be aggravated by the chaos Aquarians bring to their domestic spheres, and Aquarians are likely to find Virgos overly fussy and exacting when organizing and maintaining their homes.

Typical Aquarians are not particularly domestic and may survive on junk food, take-out, or whatever else is at hand, while Virgos tend to be finicky about food or sensitive to particular ingredients or food types. This can make it difficult for these two to establish meal routines that are satisfying for both partners.

More significant problems arise from the fact that Virgos value stability, consistency, and healthy routines, whereas Aquarians have low boredom thresholds and require regular surprises (or, in some cases, even significant upheavals) to keep them from growing restless. Virgo is likely to be distressed and destabilized by Aquarian unpredictability, while Aquarius feels oppressed by the Virgo need for consistency.

Despite their many differences, there is some common ground because both signs tend to be progressive and intellectually oriented, and they have a strong desire to help the world in some way. If their rising or moon signs are more compatible, this can be an interesting match. However, the ease with which these two can get along will depend on other elements in their natal zodiacs.

As for why Virgo men are less likely to marry Aries women while Virgo women are less likely to marry Aquarius men, gender stereotypes may play a role. Some Virgo men may have less tolerance for Aries assertiveness in women, whereas Virgo women may be more tolerant of this trait in men because society is generally more accepting of assertiveness in men.

On the other hand, Aquarian eccentricity and impracticality may be less tolerable to Virgo women than Virgo men because women have a greater need for stability in a partner. However, this is just speculation, and there may be other reasons for the gender differences in marriage rates.

Although the Virgo-Aquarius pairing, like the Virgo-Aries pairing, is less likely to make it to the altar, it has a higher likelihood of sticking. Sachs found the highest divorce rate between Virgo and Aries, whereas Virgo-Aquarius pairings were no more likely to divorce than other sun-sign pairs. However, this does not mean that all Virgo-Aries matches are doomed. There are plenty of other factors in addition to the sun sign that can improve compatibility for otherwise difficult matches, and lots of supposedly incompatible sun sign pairings make excellent marriages.

The Best Match for Virgo

The most compatible match for many Virgos of either gender is another Virgo, whereas Aries appears to be the most problematic match for Virgo men and Aquarius for Virgo women. However, Virgos who find themselves romantically entangled with one of the less compatible signs should not despair. Plenty of marriages between supposedly incompatible signs have lasted.

It is important to keep in mind that these are statistical tendencies; this does not mean that every romance between incompatible signs is doomed. For example, out of 6,498,320 marriages encompassing all possible sign combinations in the Castille study, there were 972 *more* marriages between Virgo men and Virgo women than would be expected if sun signs had no effect, whereas between Virgo men and Aries women, there were 633 *fewer* marriages than would be expected if pairings were random. However, there still were many marriages between the supposedly least compatible signs.

Astrology is complex, and there is more to consider than just sun signs. Two people with incompatible sun signs may have highly compatible rising signs or moon signs that can make the difference between a bad match and a good match with a bit of an "edge" that keeps things interesting.

*The methodology of the Sachs study has been criticized and this research continues to be controversial. I have found no critiques of the Castille study thus far.

Chapter 5: Why Some Signs Are More Compatible with Virgo Than Others

Why are some astrological signs more compatible with Virgo than others? Traditional astrologers believe that signs of the same element will be the most compatible, and that fire and air signs will be more compatible with one another, as will earth and water signs, whereas fire and air are more likely to clash with earth and water. They also believe that clashes are more likely to occur among different signs of the same quality (cardinal, fixed, or mutable).

Compatibility according to traditional astrologers:

- Virgo (earth, mutable) + Aries (fire, cardinal): very challenging

- Virgo (earth, mutable) + Taurus (earth, fixed): excellent

- Virgo (earth, mutable) + Gemini (air, mutable): very challenging

- Virgo (earth, mutable) + Cancer (water, cardinal): good

- Virgo (earth, mutable) + Leo (fire, fixed): somewhat challenging

- Virgo (earth, mutable) + Virgo (earth, mutable): excellent

- Virgo (earth, mutable) + Libra (air, cardinal): somewhat challenging

- Virgo (earth, mutable) + Scorpio (water, fixed): good

- Virgo (earth, mutable) + Sagittarius (fire, mutable): very challenging

- Virgo (earth, mutable) + Capricorn (earth, cardinal): excellent

- Virgo (earth, mutable) + Aquarius (air, fixed): somewhat challenging

- Virgo (earth, mutable) + Pisces (water, mutable): very challenging

Note: Two people who seem incompatible based on their sun signs may actually be far more compatible than expected because the elements and qualities of other placements in their natal zodiacs (ascendants, moon signs, etc.) are a much better match. See Appendix 2 for more information on this.

The Elements

The astrological elements are fire, earth, air, and water. Each element includes three of the twelve astrological signs.

Fire Signs: Aries, Leo, Sagittarius

Those who have a lot of planets in fire signs tend to be courageous, enterprising, and confident. Their love of excitement causes them take risks, and they are often extravagant or careless with money.

Fire people are generous to a fault, idealistic, and helpful. They are quick to anger, but also quick to forgive, and usually honest, in many cases to the point of bluntness or tactlessness.

Fire people are energetic and often athletic. They are assertive and (in some cases) aggressive or argumentative. Impulsivity can lead to poor decisions, financial disasters, and unnecessary conflict. Extroverted and easily bored, they seek attention and tend to be affectionate and friendly.

Earth Signs: Taurus, Virgo, Capricorn

Those who have many planets in earth signs tend to be responsible, reliable, and trustworthy. They can usually be counted on to provide stability and practical help, and they are loyal to their friends and not inclined to be fickle, though when someone crosses them, they can be quite ruthless in cutting that person out of their lives forever. Sane, reasonable, and diplomatic, those whose charts are weighted toward earth are slow to anger but also slow to forgive, and often hold grudges. However, they are usually reasonable and diplomatic unless severely provoked.

Those with a preponderance of earth signs in their charts tend to be physically strong and have great endurance. They are inclined to achieve success through hard work, and their innate cautiousness, fear of change, and need for security keep them from making rash decisions or gambling excessively, though these traits can also cause them to miss opportunities or get into ruts. While not exceptionally innovative, they have good follow-through and are able to finish what they start.

Air Signs: Gemini, Libra, Aquarius

Those who have a lot of planets in air signs tend to be intellectual in outlook rather than emotional, which can cause some to view them as insensitive. Logical, rational, and emotionally detached by nature, they can be open-minded and non-judgmental in most cases. Air people also tend to be friendly and sociable.

Air sign people are adaptable, mentally flexible, and easy going. They tend not to blow up at others in anger-provoking situations, as they are more inclined to analyze circumstances than to react passionately. They are also easily bored and require a diverse array of social companions, hobbies, and other entertainments. Air people usually love change and tend to be experimental and open to new experiences. Impulsivity and curiosity often lead them to make impractical decisions or squander their money.

Water Signs: Cancer, Scorpio, Pisces

Those who have many planets in water signs are highly intuitive and therefore able to discern the emotions, needs, and motivations of others. Water people are compassionate and inclined to care for the physically sick and the emotionally damaged. They can be very self-sacrificing on behalf of those they care for, and even in the service of strangers in some cases.

Sensitive and easily hurt, water people often develop a tough outer shell to hide their vulnerability. They are passionate in their attachments to people and prone to jealousy. Because they are idealistic, they are also inclined to gloss over the faults of others, and as a result, they can be deceived by unscrupulous people.

Water people are sensual and creative. Given the right environment and opportunity, they can produce art, music, literature, or in some cases, inventions or scientific ideas that have profound effects on others.

The Qualities

The astrological qualities are fixed, cardinal, and mutable. Each category includes four of the astrological signs.

Cardinal: Aries, Cancer, Libra, Capricorn

A person with the majority of natal planets in cardinal signs will be enterprising and inclined to initiate courses of action. Cardinal people make things happen and transform situations. This can be done to the benefit or detriment of others.

Fixed: Taurus, Leo, Scorpio, Aquarius

Those who have a lot of planets in fixed signs have good follow-through. They tend to stick to a single course of action and carry out activities to their completion or conclusion. Fixed-sign people are often moody or stubborn, and they often have intense reactions to things. However, they can act as stabilizing forces for others because they tend to behave in a consistent manner.

Mutable: Gemini, Virgo, Sagittarius, Pisces

Those who have the majority of their planets in mutable signs are flexible and adaptable. They accept change and adjust well to new circumstances that can throw other types off kilter. Mutable people are often better in a crisis than in a stable situation.

See Appendix 2 for information on how to find your other planetary placements to determine which elements and qualities are predominant in your natal zodiac.

Chapter 6: Virgo Children

Conscientious and Mature

Typical Virgo children are conscientious, helpful, and sometimes overly serious, which can make them seem older than their years. They learn quickly and rarely need to be told twice to do something. They also tend to be tidy and like to keep themselves clean.

Virgo children are unusually independent from an early age. They tend to be responsible and reliable even throughout their teen years, and many seem far more mature than their peers.

Virgo children may talk earlier than other children and go through other intellectual development stages early as well. However, they usually proceed with careful slowness when embarking on riskier physical activities (for example, learning to ride a bike or swim).

Eager to Learn

Virgo children often do well in school because they like to learn (though if they go to bad schools, they may prefer to learn on their own by reading). Many show an early talent for writing or mathematics.

Typical Virgo children work hard in school and continue to pursue lifelong learning. They also show unusual persistence when completing projects or engaging in hobbies, and their perfectionism can cause them to be very hard on themselves. They tend to judge everything they do harshly as they attempt to live up to their own unreasonable standards.

Most Virgo children love to read or have others read to them from an early age. Those who are not interested in reading will find other ways to learn new things because Virgos are knowledge seekers.

Humble and Undemanding

Virgo children are inclined to let others take credit for things and they are not prone to bragging unless their ascendants inclined them to be more self-promoting. They may not get their fair share of praise and attention because they tend to be quiet, reliable, well-behaved, and not inclined to seek the spotlight or make demands.

Virgo children will happily do their own thing unsupervised for hours on end. Preferred activities usually include crafts, building things (with blocks, LEGO, craft kits, etc.), or sorting and organizing toys or collections of objects (most Virgos like collecting and sorting things and this trait shows up early on).

Eating Habits

Virgo children are prone to food sensitivities. Their diets must be chosen carefully, or they may suffer frequent stomach upsets. Many refuse to eat certain foods.

Virgo children usually have very strong food preferences and aversions and should never be forced to eat foods they dislike, as this can lead to digestive problems and eating disorders. Adolescent Virgo girls are particularly vulnerable to eating disorders due to perfectionism and a desire to control their bodies.

Hobbies

Virgo children often have an interest in practical crafts or the natural world. Many also love anything that can be sorted, classified, or constructed.

Virgo children gravitate to toys that have educational value or that allow them to produce something tangible and that require detail work (for example, building model airplanes, beading, etc.) as opposed to toys that are used for imaginary play.

Mental Health

Virgo children are prone to worrying and can become very anxious. They are also vulnerable to becoming depressed in difficult situations.

Parents should watch closely for signs of unhappiness because Virgos tend to maintain poker faces, hiding their suffering from the world to avoid appearing vulnerable or burdening others with their problems.

Chapter 7: Virgo Parents

Virgo parents are responsible, reliable, and excellent in a crisis. They bring many strengths to parenting, including reliability, practicality, common sense, modesty, the ability to maintain a calm demeanor in stressful situations, and a talent for nursing the sick.

Virgos are also health-conscious, so they tend to feed their children nutritious foods and encourage them to exercise. They also set a good example by eating healthy foods and staying active themselves.

Although Virgo health consciousness is usually a positive trait for parenting, some Virgo parents can become so obsessive about healthy living that they do not allow their children any treats at all (in such cases, their children will usually sneak off to have these things in secret and lie about it).

Virgo parents are very good at keeping their cool (at least externally) in upsetting situations, so they are unlikely to scream at their children or humiliate them in public. They tend to be classy and in control of themselves, which provides a positive example for their children to follow.

The greatest weaknesses of Virgo parents are difficulty showing spontaneous affection in words or physical gestures and a tendency to nitpick. However, Virgo parents with more affectionate or easy going rising signs are less likely to have these problems.

Virgo parents usually provide plenty of educational toys and experiences for their children. They pass on their love of learning, improving their children's career prospects,

The children of Virgo parents can also learn from the excellent Virgo work ethic, reliability, and pragmatic approaches to problem solving. Children who emulate their Virgo parents' good qualities will be more likely to succeed in life.

Chapter 8: Virgo Health

Virgos are prone to anxiety and negative rumination, so illnesses may be triggered or worsened by unhappiness.

When Virgos are feeling good, their immune systems tend to be quite strong because they are usually bolstered by excellent health habits (unless their ascendants incline them to be more lazy or decadent). However, stress is the Virgo's Achilles heel. When under pressure, Virgos have difficulty fighting off viruses and healing from injuries.

Virgos also tend to be very sensitive to particular foods. Eating certain things can bring on stomach upsets and digestive troubles (though these may also be caused by stress). Traditional astrologers have listed bowel disorders, skin disorders (often worsened by stress), and bad nerves as common Virgo afflictions.

Market research data provided by Sachs indicates that Virgos are more likely to take painkillers for headaches than those of other signs. Virgos may get more headaches overall, or they have an average number of headaches but take painkillers to soldier on with their work, parenting duties, fitness activities, or hobbies. Headaches are often caused or exacerbated by stress, so it would be unsurprising to find that Virgos are particularly vulnerable to them.

Some Virgos are at risk for anxiety disorders or depression because they are too hard on themselves or because they are inclined toward pessimism. Working to develop a more optimistic outlook on life and more reasonable standards is beneficial for Virgos.

Virgo anxiety may also be caused by an excessive focus on bodily symptoms. Some Virgos misinterpret normal bodily signs as indicators of impending disaster and panic over them. As a result, they may become hypochondriacal, obsessively searching online for information about symptoms and their causes.

Virgos are also prone to eating disorders, particularly anorexia, because they want to control their bodies as much as possible, which can lead to rigid control of food intake. Virgos have incredible self-discipline and self-control, so they can starve themselves nearly to death if they succumb to anorexia. However, malnourishment among Virgos is not always caused by eating disorders. Some Virgos stay so busy that they simply do not have time to eat enough.

Despite their vulnerability to worry and stress, many Virgos enjoy robust health because they tend to stay active and watch what they eat. They also reduce their likelihood of injury by taking a thoughtful, cautious approach to physically risky activities (avoiding them or engaging in them with a safety-conscious attitude).

Virgo lifestyles are usually healthier than those of most people, so their health prospects are better overall. When they do suffer from ill health, it is more often due to bad luck than bad life choices, unless their ascendants incline them to be more impulsive or self-indulgent.

The most important health changes Virgos can make are taking time to relax and being kinder to themselves. Yoga, Thai Chi, and other body arts; meditation; and relaxation techniques can be helpful.

Chapter 9: Virgo Hobbies

Pastimes associated with the sign of Virgo include:

- charity or volunteer work
- cooking healthy meals and snacks
- crossword puzzles
- environmental preservation
- European football (soccer)
- gardening (particularly food gardens)
- non-team sports such as tennis, swimming, and cycling
- organizing things
- practical crafts
- reading

- researching/learning new things
- sewing
- taking care of animals
- walking, hiking, strength training, and other forms of solitary exercise
- woodworking
- writing (usually nonfiction)

Chapter 10: Virgo Careers

The earth signs do best in careers that offer security and opportunities to advance through hard work and talent rather than flashy showmanship. Taurus, Virgo, and Capricorn people work effectively either on their own or with other people, and do not require much supervision to get the job done. Most get along well with coworkers and supervisors unless severely provoked.

Earth sign people should avoid careers that involve significant physical discomfort, such as cold, wet conditions outdoors in bad climates or extreme heat unless their ascendants are in fire or air signs. Earth signs are very sensitive to aspects of the environment, so a healthy workspace with natural lighting, ergonomically friendly seating, and environmentally friendly practices is ideal.

Virgo Career Aptitudes

According to traditional astrologers, typical Virgos are good at anything involving fine detail work, numbers, research, medicine, health, or nutrition. However, they usually do well at almost anything they try because they have good work ethics, learn new skills easily, and tend to stick with things until they master them. Some Virgos are also drawn to dance or other physical arts that require intense dedication, long hours of practice, and the perfecting fine details.

Virgos have excellent organizational skills and a desire to make the world a better place through some sort of service. They are tireless workers, though they may lack the aptitude or desire for assertive self promotion. Humble Virgos do not demand much (if any) recognition because they take pride in their work rather than in what others say about their wok. Most can put in long and unpleasant hours without complaining, and they tend to be meticulous and perfectionist in everything they do.

Virgo careers and career fields, according to traditional astrologers, include:

- accountant/ bookkeeper
- analyst (financial or other)
- architect
- charity worker
- consultant
- craftsperson
- critic
- dancer
- dentist
- designer
- dietician
- doctor
- editor
- environmental organization worker
- event organizer
- gardener
- home-care worker
- inspector
- institutional worker (particularly in mental hospitals and prisons)
- interior decorator

- lab technician
- librarian
- mathematician
- naturopathic healer
- nonfiction writer (especially books on nutrition, medicine, and general health)
- nurse
- researcher
- nutritionist
- scientist
- seamstress/tailor
- secretary
- social worker
- statistician
- teacher
- translator

Chapter 11: Virgo Differences

Sachs collected a large volume of market research data for his study, and this data showed some average differences among the sun signs for certain beliefs, attitudes, interests, hobbies, activities, and preferences. The following are items for which there was a significant difference between Virgos and the sun sign average (a significantly higher or lower percentage of positive or negative responses from Virgos compared to the average for all the sun signs). Not all Virgos followed these trends; they were just more likely to match them than those of other sun signs.

Generational Attitudes

Virgos were more likely to report having similar attitudes to those of their parents. This is not surprising, given that Virgos tend to be cautious, skeptical, and not drawn to radical ideologies.

Altruism

Virgos more often described themselves as helpful. This is in keeping with the traditional astrological characterization of Virgos as altruistic helpers and caretakers who look after others in a crisis and unselfishly tend to those in need in their day-to-day lives.

Ambition

Virgos were more likely to believe that they were going to be successful. It is unsurprising that hardworking, serious Virgos would be destined for success in many cases, and Virgo ambitions are likely to be realistic unless their ascendants are in signs prone to overconfidence (Aries, Leo, or Sagittarius).

Strength

Virgos were more likely to describe their personalities as "strong." The self-assessment of strength may seem at odds with Virgo humility, caution, diplomacy, and emotional reserve. However, Virgos have impressive willpower, strength of character, and the ability to manage well in difficult situations or when plagued with anxiety. Their caution and diplomacy are not signs of weakness, but instead indicators of common sense. Virgos know that it is easier to get what they want with courtesy and tact than with force, and they are unwilling to sacrifice their health and welfare by taking stupid risks.

Virgo strength is a quiet strength because Virgos feel no need to brag or prove anything to others. They rise to challenges in times of hardship, but they do not feel the need to dominate and control those around them unless their ascendants are in more domineering signs.

Social Orientation

Virgos were more likely to say they could "easily get to know new people." This appears surprising because Virgos have traditionally been characterized as introverts. However, socially interacting with people and truly getting to know them are two different things.

Virgos may find it easier to get to know people on a deeper level because they tend to focus intensely on a small number of people they really like rather than spreading their social energies among big groups of friends, acquaintances, and strangers or pursuing the sorts of shallow, fleeting social interactions that occur at parties or nightclubs.

Virgos are also more inclined to listen to others because they do not want to be the center of attention. They prefer to let others reveal themselves first, so they are more likely to ask questions and show an interest in those they talk with rather than turning the conversation to their own beliefs, preferences, histories, and achievements.

Virgos learn about other people to determine whether they can be trusted, and they only share personal information about themselves when they have deemed the other person worthy.

Pragmatism

Virgos were more likely than average to purchase all types of insurance. This is in keeping with the traditional characterization of Virgo as practical, sensible, cautious, and smart enough to plan for various future scenarios.

Pets

Virgos were more likely than those of other signs to keep fish as pets (and second-most likely to keep birds, after Gemini). The sign of Virgo rules over small, domestic pets, so the Virgo interest in pets is unsurprising.

Office Equipment and Insurance

Virgos were more likely to give advice about office equipment and insurance, and they were less likely to give advice on beauty routines and makeup. These findings also accord with the traditional characterization of Virgo as oriented toward practical things and not interested in anything frivolous.

Politics

Virgos were more likely to say they were interested in politics, but they were less inclined to make commitments to political parties or causes. This indicates that Virgos like to stay informed, but they may avoid active political participation because they dislike the social demands of political action or prefer not to put themselves forward into the public eye unless their ascendants are in more outgoing signs.

Current Affairs

Virgos were more likely to read current affairs magazines. Virgos tend to be avid readers, and this finding is in keeping with the characterization of Virgo as interested in current, useful information rather than historical information or shallow amusements (for example, beauty routines or celebrity gossip).

Decision-Making

Virgos tend to be the sole decision makers when purchasing alcoholic beverages and insurance, and when making financial investments. This suggests that Virgos are fussy about beverages, in line with the traditional characterization of this sign as selective and discerning, and that they like to acquire financial assets and protections.

Higher Education

Sachs found that Virgos were less likely to study biology or psychology and more likely to study medicine or dentistry.

Although biology has traditionally been associated with the sign of Virgo, degrees in medicine and dentistry may support more lucrative careers, which may be why many Virgos pursue degrees in these fields.

Psychology is intangible and theoretical, so it is unsurprising that many Virgos would prefer fields such as medicine and dentistry where they can provide more hands-on, tangible help to those in need.

Jobs

Sachs found that Virgos were more likely than average to work as bricklayers, painters, metalworkers or fitters, insurance salesmen, company owners, and bookkeepers.

Bricklaying, painting, and metalwork are all tangible crafts that are well-suited to Virgo preferences, and practical Virgos are often interested in and knowledgeable about insurance.

Bookkeeping is associated with the sign of Virgo as well because Virgos tend to be good with numbers and meticulous about small details.

The higher-than-average rate of company ownership is also unsurprising. Virgos like to be in control and they are hardworking, industrious, and persistent, so they should be good at running things.

Sachs found that Virgos were less likely than those of most other signs to be self-employed. This is in keeping with the traditional astrological view that Virgos avoid unnecessary risk, and self-employment can be very financially risky.

Virgos were also less likely than average to be employed as farmers, computer scientists, musicians, further education teachers, or primary school teachers.

Farming is a risky profession because farmers are at the mercy of the weather and many other forces beyond their control, and musicians rarely make much money, so this career would be less appealing to pragmatic Virgos (though they may enjoy mastering one or more musical instruments as a hobby).

Computer science may be too intangible for Virgos, who prefer to create things they can see (for example, building work or practical crafts).

Teaching may require too much socializing for Virgos, who may not get enough time alone in this profession to recharge their social batteries. Typical Virgos also do not like to be the center of attention, so lecturing in front of a large group could be challenging. An additional problem with teaching is that teachers tend to be poorly compensated for their efforts, making this career a less practical choice.

Chapter 12: Virgo Stuff

The following things are associated with the sign of Virgo.

Metal: mercury

Gemstones: malachite, aventurine, sardonyx, peridot (August), sapphire (September)

Parts of the Body: intestines, nervous system

Number: 5

Places: Switzerland, Turkey, Greece, Crete, West Indies, Paris, Boston, Jerusalem, Reading, Heidelberg, Strasbourg

Animals: crane, stork, fox, chub fish, rainbow salmon, small domestic pets

Trees: hazel, nut bearing trees

Plants and Herbs: azalea, valerian, fennel, lily of the valley, myrtle, vine, sage, marjoram, savory, balm, caraway, fenugreek, morning glory

Colors: navy blue, forest green, earthy browns and grays, beige, tan, khaki

Patterns or Design Motifs: neutral or blending tones, uncluttered or simple/classic designs

Foods: carrot, beet, endive, hazel nuts

Other Virgo Associations

Other things (both tangible and intangible) that have been associated with the sign of Virgo by traditional astrologers include:

- analysis
- anatomy
- biology
- books (especially reference books)
- charities
- civil service organizations
- collections of small items
- crossword puzzles
- education

- health
- herbs
- hospitals
- hygiene
- labor organizations
- languages
- logic
- medicines
- microscopes
- numbers
- nursing
- nutrition
- pets
- practical clothing
- practical crafts
- public institutions
- public service
- sewing supplies
- stationary supplies
- statistics
- the intellect
- vitamins
- word processing tools
- writing tools

Appendix 1: Famous Virgos

Famous people with the sun in Virgo include:

- Adam Sandler
- Adam West
- Agatha Christie
- Alan Ladd
- Amy Poehler
- Amy Winehouse
- Anne Bancroft
- Anne of Cleves
- Anthony Weiner
- Arnold Palmer
- Arthur Godfrey
- B.B. King
- Bashar Al-Assad
- Ben Carson
- Bernie Sanders
- Beyonce Knowles
- Bill Murray
- Bill O'Reilly
- Billie Piper
- Billy Ray Cyrus
- Blake Lively
- Bob Newhart
- Bret Harte
- Brian Depalma
- Buddy Hackett
- Buddy Holly
- Cameron Diaz
- Carlo Gambino
- Charlie Sheen
- Chris Hadfield
- Chris Pine
- Chris Tucker
- Christopher Isherwood
- Claudette Colbert
- Claudia Schiffer
- Colin Firth
- Colonel Sanders
- Conrad Black
- Conway Twitty
- Corbin Bernsen
- Craig Claiborne
- D.H. Lawrence
- Damon Wayans

- Dave Chappelle
- David Arquette
- David Copperfield
- Dmitry Medvedev
- Dr. Phil McGraw
- Ed Begley Junior
- Ed Gein
- Elizabeth I of England
- Elliot Gould
- Faith Hill
- Ferdinand Marcos
- Frankie Avalon
- Freddie Mercury
- Geert Wilders
- Gene Kelly
- Gene Simmons
- George R.R. Martin
- Gloria Estefan
- Grandma Moses
- Greta Garbo
- Guy Ritchie
- H.G. Wells
- Hans Zimmer
- Harry Connick Jr.
- Hugh Grant
- Idris Elba
- Ingrid Bergman
- Ivan Pavlov
- Ivan the Terrible
- Jack Black
- Jackie Cooper
- Jacqueline Bisset
- Jada Pinkett Smith
- Jeff Foxworthy
- Jennifer Hudson
- Jennifer Tilly
- Jeremy Irons
- Jesse James
- Jessica Mitford
- Jimmy Connors
- Jimmy Fallon
- Johann Wolfgang von Goethe
- John Locke
- John McCain
- Joseph Kony
- Keanu Reaves
- Keith Moon
- Ken Kesey
- Kim Davis
- Kobe Bryant

- Lance Armstrong
- Larry Hagman
- Laura Secord
- Lauren Bacall
- Lea Michele
- Leann Rimes
- Leo Tolstoy
- Leonard Bernstein
- Leslie Jones
- Liam Payne
- Lily Tomlin
- Louis CK
- Lyndon B. Johnson
- Marco Polo
- Margaret Sanger
- Mark Harmon
- Martin Freeman
- Mary Shelley
- Maurice Chevalier
- Melissa McCarthy
- Michael Buble
- Michael Jackson
- Michael Keaton
- Mike Huckabee
- Moby
- Molly Shannon

- Mother Teresa
- Neil Peart
- Niall Horan
- Nick Jonas
- Nicole Richie
- Oliver Stone
- Patsy Cline
- Paulo Coelho
- Pink
- Pippa Middleton
- Prince Harry
- Queen Elizabeth I
- Queen Noor of Jordan
- Queen Rania of Jordan
- Quvenzhane Wallis
- Rachael Ray
- Racquel Welch
- Raymond Massey
- Regis Philbin
- Richard Gere
- Ricki Lake
- River Phoenix
- Roald Dahl
- Robert Blake

- Robin Leach
- Rocky Marciano
- Ronaldo
- Rose McGowan
- Rosie Perez
- Salma Hayek
- Samuel Johnson
- Sean Connery
- Shania Twain
- Shaun White
- Sid Caesar
- Sophia Loren
- Stephen King
- Taylor Caldwell
- Temple Grandin
- Theodore Dreiser
- Tim Burton
- Tom Hardy
- Tommy Lee Jones
- Twiggy
- Tyler Perry
- Upton Sinclair
- Warren Buffet
- Yasser Arafat

Virgo Rising (Virgo Ascendant)

The ascendant is the mask we wear in social situations, or the outer persona we show to others. In the case of Virgo rising, the external personality will be defined by Virgo traits, or a blend between Virgo and the sun sign.

Famous people with Virgo rising include:

- Agatha Christie
- Albert Camus
- Annie Lennox
- Betty Ford
- Brooke Shields
- Carol Channing
- Christina Ricci
- Conan O'Brien
- Cybill Shepherd
- David Byrne
- David Copperfield
- Dick Cheney
- Dolly Parton
- Don Johnson
- Doris Day
- Dwight Yoakam
- Faye Dunaway
- Franklin D. Roosevelt
- Gene Kelly
- George Foreman
- Harry Hamlin
- Helen Hunt
- Henry Ford II
- Hugh Hefner
- J.R.R. Tolkien
- James Taylor
- Jamie Farr
- Jeff Bridges
- Julie Andrews
- K.D. Lang
- Kathy Bates
- Kevin Costner
- Kim Carnes
- Kurt Cobain

- Loni Anderson
- Marlene Dietrich
- Oscar Wilde
- Patty Duke
- Patty Hearst
- Paul McCartney
- Paul Simon
- Placido Domingo
- Roy Orbison
- Shannen Doherty
- Sheena Easton
- Shirley MacLaine
- Sissy Spacek
- Socrates
- Ted Danson
- Tiger Woods
- Tim Robbins
- Tom Hanks
- Uma Thurman
- Walt Disney
- Warren Beatty
- Woody Allen

Appendix 2: Moon Signs, Ascendants (Rising Signs), and Planets

The natal zodiac is like a snapshot of the sky at the moment of birth. Astrologers believe that planetary placements and aspects at the time of birth influence personality and fortune. The sun, moon, and ascendant (rising sign) are the primary astrological forces, though planets also play a role.

Astrodienst (www.Astro.com) offers free chart calculation, so you can use this site to find your planetary placements and aspects and your rising sign (for the rising sign, you will need your time of birth as well as the date and place).

The Most Significant Astrological Forces

Most people know their Sun sign, which is the zodiac position of the sun at the time of birth, but few know their rising or moon signs or where their angular planets lie. In fact, the majority of people are surprised to learn that they even have these things.

Of the planetary placements, the sun, moon, and rising signs have the strongest effect on personality. The other planetary placements (positions of the planets at the time of birth) also have effects, though these are not as strong and tend to be concentrated in certain areas rather than shaping the entire personality.

The Sun Sign

The sun sign provides information about basic character and a framework for the rest of the natal zodiac. However, other elements such as the rising sign (also known as the ascendant) and moon sign affect the way the sun sign is expressed.

The Rising Sign (Ascendant)

The rising sign determines the outward expression of personality, or the way in which a person interacts with the external world. It can be described as the public persona or mask. It also indicates how an individual is likely to be perceived by others (how he or she comes across socially).

When the sun and ascendant are in the same or similar signs, a person behaves in a way that is consistent with his or her inner character. When the rising sign is very different from the sun sign, the individual is likely to be pulled in competing directions or to send out signals that don't match inner feelings, which increases the likelihood of being misunderstood by others. While such conflicts can make life difficult, they are also a source of creativity and a spur to achievement.

The Moon

The moon sign is the private persona, only seen in adulthood by those very close to the person. The moon rules over childhood and people are more likely to express their moon sign personalities when they are young. In adulthood, the moon's influence is usually hidden, relegated to the secret emotional life, though an individual may openly express the moon sign persona in times of stress or other emotional extremes.

The moon also represents the mother and other female forces in a person's life. The placement of the moon in a natal chart can indicate the types of relationships and interactions a person is likely to have with women.

Other Planets

Other planets also play a role in shaping the qualities that make up an individual. Each of the planets has a particular sphere of influence, and its effects will be determined by the sign in which the planet falls and the aspects it makes to other planets.

Mercury: all forms of mental activity and communication, including speaking and writing, the intellect, intelligence, reason, perception, memory, understanding, assimilation of information, and critical thinking

Venus: love, affection, pleasure, beauty, sex appeal, art, romantic affairs, adornment, social graces, harmony, and friendship

Mars: physical energy, will power, temper, assertiveness, boldness, competitiveness, impulsiveness, forcefulness, aggression, action, accidents, destructiveness, courage, and sex drive

Jupiter: luck and fortune, optimism, generosity, expansiveness, success, higher education, law, medicine, philosophy, abundance, and spirituality

Saturn: hard work, responsibility, character, strength of will, endurance, hard karma, difficulties, obstacles, hardship, the ability to see a task through to completion, authority, diligence, limitations, self-control, stability, patience, maturity, restriction, and realism

Uranus: progressiveness, change, originality, invention, innovation, technology, science, rebellion, revolution, sudden events and opportunities, awakenings, shocks, flashes of genius, eccentricity, unconventionality, unusual circumstances or events, independence, visionary ideas, and occult interests

Neptune: imagination, intuition, mysticism, dreams, fantasies, compassion, psychic abilities, visions, spirituality, strange events, the subconscious, repressed memories, glamour, mystery, insanity, drama, addiction, ideals, inspiration, transcendence, artistic sensibilities, and creative genius

Pluto: power, transformation, release of dormant forces, change, the subconscious, suppressed energies, death, rebirth, regeneration, sex, jealousy, passion, obsession, intensity, creation and destruction, beginnings and endings that occur simultaneously (one thing ending so that another can begin), secrets, mystery, undercurrents, precognition, personal magnetism, and extremes of personality

House Placements

House placements are a sort of fine tuning, adding some small, specific details about the ways in which various planetary placements will be expressed. The planets represent the spheres of life in which the sign traits are acted out, and the house placements are the stage or setting for these acts.

1st House: self-awareness and self-expression, outer personality, responses to outside stimuli, assertiveness, competitiveness, self-promotion, and courses of action chosen (ruled by mars)

2nd House: material possessions and attitude towards material possessions and money, ability to earn money, extensions of material wealth such as quality of food, decadence, luxury, and physical or external beauty (ruled by Venus)

3rd House: logical and practical reasoning, the intellect, agility, dexterity, curiosity, all forms of communication, all forms of media, intuition about trends and public desires or tendencies, short journeys, and siblings (ruled by Mercury)

4th House: home and hearth, domestic life, domestic chores, family, babies, comfort, the mothering instinct, food, and household items (ruled by the moon)

5th House: creative self-expression, socializing, children, early education, sports, the arts (especially the performing arts), pleasure and places of amusement, parties, social popularity, amd fame (ruled by the sun)

6th House: necessary tasks, details, health consciousness, nutrition, humility, hard work, organization, service, self-control, and sense of duty (ruled by Mercury)

7th House: relationships, friendships, marriage, all forms of partnership (business and social), harmony, balance, conflict avoidance, sense of justice, ideals, the reactions of others to our actions, what attracts us to other people (the sign at the beginning of our seventh house is often the astrological sign we find most attractive), fairness, and aesthetic sense (ruled by Venus)

8th House: legacies, shared resources, taxes, power, death, rebirth, sexuality, the dark side of life, deep psychology, personal magnetism, transformation (self-initiated or imposed by external forces), secrets or secret societies, spying, and prophetic dreaming (ruled by Pluto)

9th House: long distance travel, higher education, religion, medicine, law, animals, knowledge gained through travel and philosophical thinking, high ideals, philanthropy, luck, expansiveness, and ideas about social justice and civilization (ruled by Jupiter)

10th House: career, responsibility, honor and dishonor, perceptions of authority, relationships with authority figures, relationships with business and political power structures, responsibility, hard work, limitations, social standing, public reputation, and business (ruled by Saturn)

11th House: humanitarian endeavors, social ideals, group work, intellectual creative expression, desire to change social and political structures, contrariness, rebelliousness, invention and innovation, progressiveness, change, and personal freedom (ruled by Uranus)

12th House: the subconscious mind, self-sacrifice, intuition, miracles, secret knowledge, martyrdom, spiritual joy and sorrow, imagination, dreams, brilliance, madness, sensation-seeking, self-destruction, addiction, compassion, kindness, the ability to transcend boundaries, confusion, deception (of others and oneself), and altruism (ruled by Neptune)

Angular Planets

Angular planets are planets located along the axis – in other words, planets that fall along the line where the 12th house joins the 1st house, the 3rd house joins the 4th house, the 6th house joins the 7th house, and the 9th house joins the 10th house. Of these, the line that separates the 12th house from the 1st house and the line that separates the 9th house from the 10th house are considered the most important.

Planets that fall where the 12th house joins the 1st house will have a particularly strong effect on overall personality. Planets at this location are called rising planets, so a person with Uranus on the cusp of the 12th and 1st houses will be strong in the areas ruled over by Uranus and show traits of the sign that Uranus rules (Aquarius).

Planets located on the midheaven, which is the cusp of the 9th and 10th houses, also have a very strong effect on certain aspects of personality, particularly career aptitudes and choices. Rising and midheaven planets are some of the most important factors in a person's chart, though IC planets (those located on the cusp of the 3rd and 4th houses) and descending planets (located on the cusp of the 6th and 7th houses) can also have an effect.

The IC provides insights into the self that is seen by those closest to us, such as family, as well as our family structure.

The descendant, or cusp of the 6th and 7th houses, indicates the sorts of people we are attracted to. Theoretically, we should be most attracted to the sign of our descendant (directly opposite our ascendant).

Some astrologers believe that people who have many angular planets are more likely to become famous at some point during their lives.

Aspects

Aspects are the angles the planets formed in relation to one another at the time of a person's birth. The aspects considered most important include the conjunction, sextile, square, trine, inconjunct, and opposition.

Conjunction

A conjunction occurs when two planets are 0 degrees apart – in other words, right next to one another. This powerful aspect is often beneficial, though not always, because if the two planets involved are in negative aspect to many other planets, the conjunction can intensify the problems associated with the difficult aspects.

Planets in conjunction are working together, and their influence will have a major effect on personality. People with planets in conjunction often have one or two extremely well-developed talents or aptitudes, and many people who invent things or are responsible for medical breakthroughs have conjunctions or stelliums (more than two planets in conjunction). Having three or more planets in conjunction can indicate genius in a certain area.

Sextile

A sextile occurs when two planets are 60 degrees apart. Sextiles are beneficial aspects that create opportunities.

Unlike the trine, which simply drops good fortune in a person's lap, the sextile presents opportunities in the areas ruled by the planets involved in the sextile, and it is up to the individual to seize these opportunities and make something of them.

Square

A square occurs when two planets are 90 degrees apart. Squares are stressful or challenging aspects.

Having squares in a natal chart often encourages creativity and ambition, as squares bring obstacles that must be overcome and strife that inspires the individual to develop necessary strengths and use creative problem solving abilities. Squares can promote character development because they ensure that life never becomes too easy.

Trine

Trines occur when two planets are 120 degrees apart. Trines are the most positive and harmonious aspects, bringing good fortune, ease, advantage, and luck in the areas ruled over by the planets involved in the trine.

Inconjunct

An inconjunct occurs when two planets are 150 degrees apart. The effects of the inconjunct are unpredictable, though often problematic.

An inconjunct can indicate stress, health problems, weaknesses, challenges, and obstacles in the personality or the environment that must be overcome. Some astrologers believe that the inconjunct (also known as a quincunx) brings the type of challenges that create wisdom.

Opposition

An opposition occurs when two planets are 180 degrees apart. Oppositions are difficult aspects that can bring discord, stress, chaos, and irritation, but like squares they tend to promote creativity, strength, and character development. It is more productive to view them as challenges rather than problems.

References

Bugler, C. (Ed.). (1992). *The Complete Handbook of Astrology*. Marshall Cavendish Ltd., Montreal.

Castille, D. (2000). *Sunny Day for a Wedding*. Les Cahiers du RAMS.

Fenton, S. (1989). *Rising Signs*. HarperCollins, London.

Heese, A. (2017). Cafe Astrology. CafeAstrology.com.

Quigley, J.M. (1975). *Astrology for Adults*. Warner Books, New York.

Rowe, P. *The Health Zodiac*. Ashgrove Press, Bath.

Sachs, G. (1998). *The Astrology File: Scientific Proof of the Link Between Star Signs and Human Behavior*. Orion Books, London.

Woolfolk, J.M. (2001). *The Only Astrology Book You'll Ever Need*. Madison Books, Lanham, MD.

Image Credits

Virgo glyph: Peter-Lomas, Pixabay, https://pixabay.com/en/virgo-astrology-sign-symbol-2552259/

All other images were found on http://www.publicdomainfiles.com

- A pair of hearts: Mogwai
- Alianças (rings): Adassoft
- Beets: Lance Cheung, USDA
- Book stack: Cyberscooty
- Business people silhouettes: Asrafil
- Cockatiel: Karen Arnold
- Faces: Inky2010
- Father walking with his children: CDC/Amanda Mills
- Fox: Kristine Sowl, US Fish & Wildlife Service
- Hands with hearts: Petr Kratochvil
- Jigsaw: Yuri1969
- Love of books: George Hodan
- Morning glory flower: Petr Kratochvil
- Night sky with moon and stars: George Hodan
- Penguins: Merlin 2525
- Stethoscope: Johnny_automatic
- Young girl playing on the beach: Amanda Mills, CDC

Made in the USA
San Bernardino, CA
08 February 2019